Learning to Breathe

John Gilham

Stairwell Books
//,

Published by Stairwell Books
70 Barbara Drive
Norwalk
CT 06851 USA

161 Lowther Street
York, YO31 7LZ

ISBN: 978-1-939269-37-9

Printed and bound in UK by Russell Press
Layout design: Alan Gillott
Cover photograph: John Gilham

Acknowledgements

The following poems have been published previously:

First Publication.

"Happiness", "View from the Hills", "Queuing for Churchill…", "Inside the Beltway" and "Hurtling South" in *Acumen 72, 62, 81 and 79 (2)* respectively.

"Standing Further Back", "A Window on the World", and "The Minster Fire" in *Aireings 42, 47, and 45* respectively.

"Barefoot in the Dark" and "Out of Sight, Out of Mind" in *Dream Catcher 9* and *24* respectively.

"Chivalry", "School Trip…", "Hardy Revisited", "Biking Through Michigan", "Almannagja…", "Farmer", "Mordred's Tale","The 78", "Rights of Way", "The Boundary" and "Offstage" in *Pennine Platform 76 (2), 75 (2), 77, 68, 64, 72(2) 60 (2)* respectively.

"Love Poem" in *The Rialto 45*.

"The Underground" in *Aesthetica 16*.

"Wild West (Telemark)" in *Poet in the Round 2*.

"Easter Frost" in *The Affectionate Punch 13*.

Anthologies

"The Minster Fire", "Out of Sight, Out of Mind" and "Skeletons" in *York 800, ed. Coopey and Guthrie, pub'd. Stairwell Books.*

"A Window on the World" in *Along the Iron Veins, ed. Gillott and Drew. Pub'd. Stairwell Books.*

"Myth-making" in *The Green Man Awakes, ed. Drew. Pub'd. Stairwell Books.*

"Barefoot in the Dark", "The Underground" and "Wild West (Telemark)" in *The Exhibitionists, ed Drew and Gillott. Pub'd. Stairwell Books.*

For Carol, with thanks.

Table of Contents

View from the Hills

There are visions, and re-visions
and we begin to see, not clearly
but across a landscape dashed with showers,
splashed with sunlight,
a sketch, pencilled in the haze of distance
of what might be a destination.

There are advances and retreats
but overall, peacefully,
building a bridge here, filling a trench there
and by sowing crops
(which very action is a kind of promise)
we build a country we can grow in
reaching towards a city
that might be home. ⁄⁄

Homecoming

We were blown off course;
we tangled in the skerries off Scotland,
till I thought we were drowned;
we lost oars against the rocks, rigging,
everything but ourselves in that sharp arena.

And as we struggled, you stabbed;
you in the short days and you in the lash of the rain,
when every East wind that flung through the fjord
piled the sea against hope;
the old talkers mouthed nothings in the long nights.

We lost direction.
I tied everyone to his bench and me to the stern-post
and we rode the mountains - and slept.
It's never impossible to sleep.
Even you slept sometimes - when the wind
whipped so strong it cut scars in the rock
even you slept, for all seemed final then ...

Until we woke up, the salt cracking our faces,
and the low sun focusing the cold.
The odds were suddenly worth rowing for;
we cast lots for the oars.

You looked out through the islands,
you saw the steel chop of the waves;
and the snow line crept lower behind you;
someone's wife embraced a new lover;
someone's son took someone's wife;
and each night the stars grew more bitter
as you watched them in the South;
and we watched them too, and it was late.

We had to beat up against the cold,
sheltering between islands,
local fishermen grudging us scraps.
The sea froze on our oars, and we thought, inside,
of the stuffy huts' thick atmosphere of wives and relatives
and our backs creaked. Surprised seabirds mocked us,

mocked our muscles as we rowed without ceasing
until fast in a rhythm of islands we were gripped by the fog
- you thought it a shroud.

The old ones expected no portent;
they stood on the shore, gossiping into emptiness
like lighthouse voices of the dead -
until you made us; out of some cloud gave form
to this chance coherence of sea-mist molecules;
the almost-sleeping bird appeared on the water, all undreamed,
and scattered the ghosts that hovered on the sea.
I rose, a vapour cast in a cold shroud,
and plunged, swam, to clasp your liquid kisses
tight to the memory of my arms,
as the world dissolved.

At last, lost in the home-fjord, the sea is calm.
The mist-torn mind trawls, drags through its own still waters,
and casts forth into a darkness so deep and raging
no ripple need ever break or new sun rise,
no purpose scoriate the fjord in bright ships
or ever end repeal this long still storm. ✍

Wild West (Telemark)

There was a wind.
It had spikes of rain in it.
Our destination was an act of faith.

Snow clung to the peaks,
away from where the sun might shine;
we waited while the lake chopped,
brown and grey.

And then there was a boat
that we smashed across the waves in,
bow high, engine screaming
cast upon the captain's mercy,
a mini-cab lumberjack.
We clung to trust.

And then there was a church, on an island,
where we justified our journey - candles, warmth,
and the extraordinary sound of music:
wild fiddlers from wild uplands,
celebrating a birthday,
the power of faith and family,
the spirit of a hard place,
an island in an iron lake, cold, bleak,
and next to God. //

Mordred's Tale

Merlin has a lot to answer for:
for Merlin foretold me;
and Merlin it was who whispered in my father's ear
that all his kingdom, feasts and brawls

would crumble for his tumble in his sister's bed.
He panicked. Twenty years off at least
from when I might be bold and bad enough
to end the fairytale,

Dad asked the new priest, and, given precedents,
massacred the innocents;
set them in a leaky boat upon a winter sea
and yet, old fool, missed me.

I humoured all his childish games,
his Table Round, his fighting thegns.
I let him pretend abductions, rapes, adultery
would form a story men would tell and bards would sing;

and then I watched the new religion, Merlin dead,
steer towards the sublimating Grail,
which sapped that noble fellowship of jousts
with prayer and fading visions in the mist.

Now I, who 'scaped infanticide, bide my time.
Incest's child, I shall come to my father's kingdom
through blood and fire.
I
won't inherit
by hanging on a cross. ⁄⁄

5

Chivalry

Don't disrespect the Round Table Boys,
a lot of cool, a lot of noise,
they'll joust upon an imagined slight,
their weapons sharp, their armour bright.

Honour, status, revenge and pride,
mental cues for homicide;
don't eye their bitch, their damosel,
they'll challenge you, so arm you well.

The hot wired car, the stolen gun
the wrap-round shades, they're number one;
the loyalty to class, to gang,
the hunt, the sex, prove they're a man.

The enchanted sword that wins the day,
the knife outside the take-away. //

Myth-making

I saw the blow that finished him
but cannot write too nearly of such things.
I need a little time, a chance to find again
the silence at the land's core, to focus memory,
to lose the crash of battle,
the blood hammering in my ears
the singing in the victor's halls;
to forget the women wailing and the
strong men's voices edged with tears.
Now, I seek the still point.

I wait - to render happenings as they were,
not tinged with self or passing things;
I await remembrance through the eye of truth.

Yet what chance I - if I relate
they took him to a lake
grey between mountains, racked with trees,
and heaped him in a boat that leaked and swayed,
and laid his sword and crown upon his chest,
and pushed him out so
long before the middle of the lake,
the rotten hulk, beneath its one-man royal crew
had sunk and taken Arthur to the mud,
the fishes and the worms.
Four agèd women watched him go.

What chance have I with this?

Why, even when I passed the nearest hall
not half a day from there
the tale had grown -
and men there told me he was decked in pomp
with all his noble knights surviving stood nearby,
while a royal barge, crewed by four fair queens
with king and all had vanished in a mist.
They told me he would come again.

They asked about his sword and crown.
I told them as the boat went down
the sword had slipped and plunged into the lake
the rich hilt first.

And do you know, high in a hill fort,
on the western way, just five hours hence
they told me that a man had seen
the fairest one of those same fair queens stand
and hurl King Arthur's sword across the lake
and saw a hand, as of some lady of the deep
rise from the water, seize the hilt
and wave the bright blade slowly in a long farewell.

Such is the tide of time:
the poem in men's minds becomes the truth
and what we wish had happened, did.
Men write proofs, to prove it so;
we tell you what you need to hear,
which then is. ⁄⁄

Boxing Day

On this bleak hill, flakes of ice in the wind,
the sun focusing the cold, out walking on Boxing Day,
we sheltered in the ditch of an earthwork,
huge and ancient, silted beneath the drift of centuries.
I wondered what it was for;
not just to eat one's sandwiches in
but to contain things, or keep things out,
dreams and enemies, Picts and Danes.

The landscape moves on, cows graze and forests grow
the plough erodes, lives change
and under it all the curve of the earth
its surface a palimpsest, a maze.

Today there is the silence of the season,
the world, celebrant, on pause
but through and beyond that, from the hills ahead
an axe, shaving at the wilderness
shading to a pick, a plough, a harrow
and a sweeping of scythes.

Order in the high fields
where a warrior from the past and before that
heir of the Romans yet, in his thickest blood
heir of the land before the Romans came
Arthur, twice lord, reigns on his sheep-grazed hill,
last hammer of the English, forged by the hand of God
and thrust in the fire against them
he waits with his war-band the hour of need,
and holds by the grace of the King and his will
this land together, clamped to his careful course
like roots to rock.
Who fights for the feel of the land, since he must;
ordained by the gift of the Grail,
and by acclamation of the rocks and trees.

Who knows what Arthur takes to the Grail,
who knows what faith he gives, blood he offers
and what strength given to that holy bowl
by the curve of the hill, his land and ours.

At peace, we amble where he strode
his legacy our present,
his vision ours if we care to see;
sun, friendship, our feet on the ground
the mist-veiled fields and woods of England ours
these clods the seal on the charter;
and though the purpose of this Ring eludes us, the map no help
our function is to walk cheerfully,
accepting that the gift of God is the land and the people
and the voices whispering through the last leaves.

We wind down the bright fieldside
snow beneath the hedges,
the ancient forest turned to hedged fields,
our future built on his, our eyes, our hearts
lifted to the silver slant of the winter sun
till, back in the village, we kick
the drifts of white from our boots
and find in the warmth of friends and jokes
and drinks by a fire, another bedrock
balance to the past,
a human counter to the world of myth.

We lift the glass not the Grail cup,
our vision in each other's hearts
not in some cold chapel by a winter sea,
and though we are heirs of Arthur, visions of Merlin,
neither will come again;
we must cut our own ditches, turn our own sod
and sow our own seed;
our children's fields "not ours to till,
whose weather is not ours to rule." ⁄⁄

Iona

Had you heard this?
that Christ will come again
as a woman, to Iona?

It has been said -
the idea lives out there
in the world of stories
like Arthur and the Grail
a seed in the mist.

As a woman, she would be
more frightening than He is now;
Judgement Day would be a worry.
I'd want to please her more,
mind more if she frowned.
I'd want to be able to look in her eyes.
I'd feel betrayed
if she took up with sinners and publicans.

My life would be scoured,
affections racked,
sleep shot with fear;
her eyes would burn deeper, brook no reply.

Naked, I'm not man before this woman
but human before a god:
joy of my heart or no
desire of my loins or no
she accepts no flattery,
succumbs to no charm,
and leans on no shoulder.

After her agony, if she asks,
I will love her, as a duty,
until the end of passion -
desire crucified. ✍

St. Cuthbert Comes to Crayke

St. Cuthbert came to Crayke
and turned back. Not immediately:
his old bones needed to rest; his monks,
driven by fear, and reverence, were tired;
the North was aflame.

South, times were uncertain,
Ouse and Trent like Viking arrows
aimed into Deira, Mercia. Few in that cortege
had crossed Humber or followed the roads
to London, Canterbury, perhaps safety.

Here, in this last outpost of the gilded North
the books too took rest. Too much travelling
risks the Word, risks the rich covers,
their gold and jewels temptation
for heathen footpads on the road.

In the end, bearing what they knew to be
incorrupt, holy, with all its treasures,
they took Cuthbert back across the Tees
to Wearside, to unaccustomed, perhaps unwanted,
worship and magnificence. ⁄⁄

Almannagja, Thingvellir, Iceland

There's a pool where the plates divide:
here Eurasia, there America,
different rocks, different strata.

A short rope's length away
is where they did justice,
and made laws. Everyone came,

trekking across lava fields,
fording cold rivers, sailing, rowing,
following the black coast.

They bought, they sold, they settled old feuds;
arranged marriages, determined lawsuits,
traded horses, decreed punishments,

dragged the adulteress, the infanticide,
bound, to the ritual pool, to drown
where the world comes apart;

the rift ever pregnant
with magma's overmastering flood. ⁄⁄

West Flanders

I imagine it to be flat.
I imagine the ridges to be like the eskers around York,
rising but a little above the plain, bearing a village, or a church.
There will be woods squared off by tracks and ditches
and ruled fields with crosses in straight lines.

Over a hundred years imagination blends
with the memories of those who were there,
the pictures, the poems,
and the collective, conscious
memorialization of the death of millions;
their dead our dead, our dead theirs.

Still, that war hits home - my grandfather, yours.
Still those elderly spinsters of my childhood
mourning their unlost virginity
cradling who knows what bitterness;
and the great Home on the hill now empty,
all its cripples dead at last,
so we don't have to pass by and remember.

And yet we do. That war above all
shocks still. Our eyes still weep
our wonder still grows, appalled.
It does not fade, nor become veiled.

The Holocaust was not,
or not in the same way, our holocaust.
Passchendaele was, and Ypres, and Pilckem Ridge.
Our genocide, or suicide, was on the Somme,
and now our images are mud, and poppies
and a hand reaching for the butterfly
snared on the wire.

If I were ever asked to show
what wound most scars this country's soul,
still, I would show this. ⁄⁄

Bicycling towards Ieper
(i.m. Käthe Kollwitz, sculptress)

Bicycling towards Ieper
across the small, significant, ridges of Flanders,
I found the quiet cemetery at Vladslo.

Here was a grove of trees
which in late November carried still
the memory of summer;
leaves fell on the incised names -
Johannes, Martin, Hans
- yellow on the grey slabs.

A grove where no birds sang
and Kollwitz' silent parents,
wracked with grief, mourned for us all.

To Tyne Cot and Passchendaele I carried them with me.

And years later, in the gallery, in Berlin,
I realised her cruel fate,
whose imagination was tortured,
years before the war, with images of mourning,
of mothers whose hearts were torn from their bodies
as their sons' entrails, and her son's, were torn from theirs.

Her soul, her hands knew
long before that last wave
at the corner of the street
that it would come to this unbearable quiet
this bitter hush.

How could she let him go ? ⁄⁄

Jelly's Hollow

Mother wanted me to move in.
She said he'd come soon enough
when he found no-one up at the Hollow.

But I wouldn't. Although it was hard
chopping the wood, fetching the water,
making do on his soldier's pay,

I wanted to be there, under the hill,
for when he would lope again down
the old track, kicking the leaf mould,

carrying his pack in that jaunty way,
letting the deep woods ease his memories
of splintered trees and men.

He opens the gate, approves my flowers,
my vegetables, the bushes in fruit,
he opens the door: "Hallo, gel. I'm back."

That's my story. Long after the telegram,
long after the parcel of mud-stained khaki,
the bloody shirt, my creased last letter,

that's the story I long to tell,
the story his child would love to hear. ⌗

The Best Medicine

Humankind cannot stand too much reality. T.S. Eliot.

When I told the story of how I nearly drowned
in treacherous tides off a Welsh beach,
and shouted "help, help !" before I saved myself -

my children laughed.

And once, at school, our history teacher
showed the newsreel of the airship blazing
while the commentator cried hysterically.

We laughed.

He stopped the film.
He went berserk. "Unfeeling sods" he called us.
I know what he meant.

Chaplin made us laugh at Hitler, and for all the Littlewood play
wraps war in music-hall and jokes
I don't - having seen the killing fields,

and outside the Star and Garter home
the amputees, propped at their wheelchair view
of endless sunsets over Surrey, Middlesex,
now saved from the Hun.

Scant recompense.

But then, the shell-shocked, the twitching,
the funny walks, the comic smile, the tragic mask,
the beyond imagining pain and loss
we could not comprehend, and so

we children laughed.

Forgive us. Too much reality. ⁄⁄

To the Stars

Time was, we'd go to 'The Airport'.
A bus to somewhere else would drop us
and we'd walk between the wartime huts
towards the runway, anticipating.

If you waited they'd open a gate
and you could cross the tarmac
to stand behind a fence and see
the aeroplanes come and go.

There were ice-creams, and pony rides,
and every ten or fifteen minutes
a DC3 or 4, Elizabethan, Constellation,
would roar on by and up, up and away.

My grandfather liked to come.
He'd walk beside the pony and remember
how, before, there'd been a village here -
Heathrow.

Older, I'd cycle there and through the tunnel,
and watch from the Queen's Building
the Viscounts, Comets, pirouette and dock,
marshalled by men with bats.

And then, one day, in '61
two boys cycled out and waited there
until the Bentley, open-top, appeared,
and seeing us, two lads, waving,
he stood, and waved back, just to us.

Gagarin, the first man in space.
This world a spaceport to the stars.
No limit to our journeyings.
No more pony rides. ⁄⁄

22nd November 1963

The Thames, black in the November night,
the tide ebbing, the eddies, the undertow,
the silent, deadly, swallowing of light;
and back home, Dallas, flickering on the tele.

It's not the sniper's bullet nor the madman's gun
I fear. It's the drag, the transparent slide
of fast water, the quiet depths of the unfenced dock,
the unheard cries, the treachery of tides,
the shifting planes below the weir,
the roil in the lock, the Strid,
the mill race, the devouring flood,
the red behind the eyes, the last bubble in the lungs.

A President always fears the tightened crook of a finger.
But for me, forever, it's the slip at the edge,
the tip over the balustrade, the trip on the towpath,
the attracting black oblivion on a November night. ⁄⁄

Queuing for Churchill, January 1965

There was a lot we didn't know.
There always is, until they release the papers,
with their bitter truths.

His story was not yet smudged;
the occupying forces still in place,
the legacy of Yalta not yet become blame.

London on a cold damp night,
Lambeth Embankment six deep,
the Thames tide high, empty lighters going down,

and the queue shuffling across the bridge, slow and quiet.
No need to control this crowd,
used to queuing on more cratered streets than these.

And after some hours, into the Hall:
the dark coffin, the soldiers at 4 corners.
Thanks. Respect. Tears. Awe. Salutes.

And the State Funeral. The flags,
the horses, the gun carriage, slow marching, the city,
the flotilla on the tideway, the special train.

Hard to imagine now, that so many
wept. The national story then
left no room for questions, cynics, shades of truth.

These generations had seen it all:
the smoke and rubble in the morning,
the sirens every night, the darkened streets.

The privations, the black-market,
the doodle-bugs, the V2s, the shelter's damp,
the speeches, the V-sign, the cigar. ⁄⁄

The Pigeon Lofts

I. Gateshead

Sometimes, as I pass,they're strutting,
fanning their tails, puffing their chests,
pecking, billing, cooing.

At other times, the lofts seem abandoned,
doors hanging off, unpainted additions,
a few feathers caught in the wire.

And once, from the train, I saw four blokes
drinking tea in the sunshine,
packets of biscuits, open, half-empty.

Today a man knelt on a roof,
hammering down plastic; protection
from rain, from cats, from urban foxes.

II. The Side Gallery, Newcastle

And then, across the river to an exhibition -
war photos of the ghetto in Lodz,
ghetto policemen, chests out, proud,

fences for protection, kids playing, and girls
dressed for a wedding, children for a birthday
- smiles for the camera, cakes, table-cloths, flowers.

Their smiles paper over truth;
tea-parties co-exist with the routine deaths,
the fecal duties, the hangings, the deportations.

None of these birds will fly;
huddled on trains they are not released,
they do not head home. ✍

The 78

Harbour water, unmoved by tide or current,
warehouses, cranes, cobbles.

In the films, there's a light
reflected like grease across the water
and we pan in to a cheap bar as
a voice sings low onto the soundtrack
of loss, of love, and then louder,
rough as the audience we now see through the smoke,
who talk, ignore the emotion wrung
from a cheap microphone, from battered speakers
on a beer-crate stage.

We know this child, this waif, she
who will one day be Piaf, Bassey, or Marlene,
who will take the hard dreams of this hard town
and live them, with every thrust of passion
a body can give, freed from its roots,
so that what is remembered is not that hope and ambition
used to die here nightly, but that hope lives on.

Here in the bar, where it began, hope lives, just.
Among the tourists and the nostalgia slummers
hope adds its name to the false gods and prophecies,
to alcohol, tobacco, to ecstacy, to crack,
to a belief, against the odds, in songs of love. //

Foundlings (Coram's Field, Bloomsbury, London)

1.

A wooden doll in the museum case,
a knitted cap, a button;
mothers' remembrances
their children never saw.

Some were born poor, some bastards,
and the Coram's were kind
as kindness went those days;
but never passed on those tokens;
nothing to say "you had a mother, once,"
that once you were loved.

And yet, such trifles
might have been the only
evidence of love they ever had.

And how else do you learn to love
but being loved yourself?

2.

"He will be called for again!
This scrap of cloth his mark,
and mine, who keep the like.

What though you change his name,
what though he'll suck from other breasts than mine,
what though I know how many foundlings die,

how few are ever restored or sought.
Keep this child safe.
He will be called for again." ⁄⁄

Son

nobody comes
nobody comes

there's a shiny floor
a cracked ceiling
cot bars
and sunshine
in another world

but nobody comes

someone is crying
someone is washing dishes
people are talking
somewhere
someone is crying
I am crying

nobody comes

somebody comes
somebody smiles
somebody talks

too late

I am not crying now
the hurt heals itself
scabs over

those who come
may come and go
the sun shines now
in my world, and your world
I smile, I talk
but you don't share
my world behind bars //

Castaway

Imagining a treat,
my little-known father set me adrift -
a small boat on a large pond.

I was too small:
I couldn't reach the pedal with my foot
and when I did, down beneath the dashboard,
I couldn't see.

I felt a fool. I chugged around the pond,
uncomfortable, alone, and staring at the sky
while he and Mother talked, ignoring
my attempts at coming closer.

"Watch me!" I cried, desperate,
while they, saying whatever lovers
long and still estranged, do say,
hurried, with one eye on the clock,
till I came in again;
their time was up
- I am still floundering. //

Dad

The ruined church still has a graveyard.
I find related stones:
a son dead at 2, his father 32,
a year later.

What tale, I wonder, decays there ?
What accident, what guilt,
what broken heart,
what loss of will ?

You died for me when I was 6,
the birthday cards stopped then;
maybe the love did too.

What stories fester in our past,
buried, unmarked?
Did you ever kiss me, hold me?
What does the bond of blood mean ?
Who walked away from whom ?
Did you deny me as I do you ?

Did you ever ask these questions too ?
The answers now beyond the grave. ⁄⁄

"How's Dave"

"How's Dave," she'd say,
hoping to show an interest,
thinking of me, my life.

"Mother, it's forty years,
a school friend, we lost touch. "
"Well, Bernard, then."
"Same thing."

They live on, polite boys.

Our own children tell us little,
are jealous of their friendships,
surprised if their friends ask about us,
short, if we ask about them.

We are superceded. It's not us they ask
to help move furniture; it's not us who shares
their long weekends in Paris or Berlin.

But sometimes, their friends pass by
for a cuppa and a chat; sometimes, unaccompanied,
they come to stay.
Their friends are a gift they can't take back.

It wasn't like that, then.
My mother adds it to her
pile of sadness. ⁄⁄

November

November,
when the nets of my mother's spare room,
white against the sky,
trap a black flake, ragged,
that proves a butterfly, wings folded:
caught, I guessed, last summer,
died, and left untouched,
a perfect silhouette,
that suddenly now moved,
spread its wings in colour,
climbed an inch or two, stopped,
folded, resumed its death mask –
and minutes later fluttered up, then down,
striving towards the light,
the little-did-it-know-it cold and raw, outside,
its desire frantic, its place, not in a room.

I let it out.

November.

Thus I released its soul.
Thus my mother flutters feebly,
long past her summer.
Her place is a room, still,
not ready to move on.

Perhaps for us the metaphor turns round:
we pass from life to moments in the sun,
our souls seeking a world to spread their wings,
to escape from the nets, the cold,
to be reborn more beautiful than we will ever know.

The sun descends toward the solstice.
My mother's house grows cold and dark. ⁄⁄

Mother

nobody comes

there's a shiny floor
a cracked ceiling
a high bed
curtains
somewhere, still, sunshine

nobody comes

someone is moaning,
someone is clattering bedpans,
nurses are talking
somewhere
someone is dying
I am dying

nobody comes

somebody comes
somebody smiles
somebody talks

too late

I am still dying
the hurt will not heal now
too late for the words
I still can't say

those who come
may come and go
I breathe, I remember
and night falls
nobody comes
I left you alone
I know now - abandonment breeds ⁄⁄

Offstage

At O level, we were led to Agincourt
like beasts to the slaughter.
Thoroughly, painfully,
poetry, drama, beauty
were severed from the text
and we were thrust into the breach –
the English dead -

but yet – it lives.

How many times a day
do the bard's words ring true
from "fie, wrangling queen" (Antony & Cleopatra)
to "something rotten" (Hamlet)
or "great thing of us forgot" (Lear).

So, visiting my mother dying,
who talked inconsequentially,
and fumbled with her sheets,
Shakespeare had been there, seen that,
honed the metaphor:
for her "nose was as sharp as a pen" (Henry V),
and her subsequent passing, therefore, not unheralded. ⁄⁄

Saying Goodbye

blackberry weather, fields and hedges
stretching out to the sunlit Wolds
and you, pregnant, on the tandem
waiting for our son

and then later with a child-seat,
on expeditions, walks, paddling,
or raspberry picking, tree-climbing

it worked hard, many days, to school
and then, when the kids could pedal too,
to swimming, horse riding
- chatting on the way - sociable times

and lately, creaking, erratic, retired almost,
an eccentric steed for daughter and boyfriend
cementing something in shared adversity

now, our final journey, me,
stately and slow, relieved, passing it on,
to be restored and blest

how come I felt more sad
at my last ride on this family friend
than scattering my mother's ashes
around the honeysuckle, brambles,
lush grass of that green lane,
nettles, hawthorn, sloes and crabs
the tandem missing from our gathered midst

it shared twenty-six years of growth
as she did not, who rode alone, shared little,
preserved her privacy, paid for her mistakes -
at what high cost

unfilial to mourn the tandem more. ⁄⁄

The Legacy

Sixty years on and more,
we die without knowing our fathers
or for some, our real mothers.
Perhaps, on the edge of memory
they linger, someone,
a shadow, a solace
before whatever came after,

when some were taken by the nuns
who never cared for the fruit of sin;
some were shipped like convicts,
put to work in dust and dirt,
abused and beaten,
child victims of the export trade;
many, child victims of the war,
in a world that punished
the innocent for innocence.

Conceived and born like them
on the wrong side of convention,
how close did I come
to Australia?
Whose decision to keep me on
in a suburban street ?
Whose compassion ?
And why me? ⁄⁄

Going Back

Can I ever go back ?
back before the hard choices
or the easy answers.

Back to where I was a child,
back to walk the old street,
to see the old house,
to wonder what unfinished business
brought me there,
what catharsis,
what necessary expiation.

For how did the laburnum trees
along the street
the singing teacher opposite,
the kind, sad, neighbours
come to be *my* world ?
whose choice, or whose inertia?

Not mine, a toddler;
I had no questions,
made no distinction
between what was or what might have been;
not a victim, not exiled,
perhaps, against the odds,
loved.

One parent short of a family,
two parents short of an explanation,
too many years too late
to choose knowing
having chosen not to:

the easy answer. //

Out of Sight, Out of Mind

Needing foundations for our new kitchen, we excavate.
Tiles, pottery, small bones - chicken probably -
but not till we dig a metre or so do they appear, like sticks,
and then that strange twist, ulna and radius;
and wary scraping reveals a ball and socket.
Panicked, we call in archaeologists.

The past, it seems, underpins us.
Once a courtyard where they threw scraps,
and swept out the breakage;
and before that, for centuries, a cemetery
stacked deep and close as though our kitchen
was an altar, some holy shrine to
gods of home and hearth.

Who they were we shan't know,
although we depend upon them,
as I depend upon my father, whom I hardly knew,
unearthed in a single photograph.
Not much foundation really for a family.
His very existence
a skeleton cupboarded so long;
but now no longer out of sight,
nor out of mind; roots, bones. //

Skeletons

Most families, I thought, kept them in cupboards;
most families, I thought, fed them with worry;
and most families know each time they pass that door
what lies inside it. Most families I thought
bring them out shyly, proudly, for people they trust.
How it should be.

But not in the open, everywhere.
Dig down a little round here and you'll find
one, or two, perhaps a cluster, promiscuous in death.
A bloke I know has a dozen under his kitchen,
and there's one in the basement of a house near here;
we might have a hundred between front gate and back fence,
waiting to sell their stories: conquest,
settlement, quiet enjoyment, dusty death –
and what else in between ? in our house ?

Burying one's own is one thing.
Living on top of other people's private plot
is one skeleton too many – a sudden weight of history
I hadn't bargained for when I took out the mortgage. ⁄⁄

The Minster Fire

Funny, how we missed it – that night
cycling home from the pub, so late
that on the quiet roads a barn owl flew with us,
and the night was soft like silk, tossed lightly
over woods and fields till the next long day.

And warm, the summer lightning flittering noiselessly
on all the hills around, miles distant,
and never a thunderbolt, never the heavens split
by the surgical strike we did not see,
could not remember, waking to the gutted transept,
firemen, the world's press, the finger of God. ⚡

The Fascinator

after the races
a few Pimms to the wind
they totter
in bright skimpy dresses
in six-inch heels
in platforms
and fascinators
- feathers and foil
silk and sinamay
all adroop
all askew
soggy in a summer shower

me, I bike past
in fluorescent cape
and floppy hat

they laugh
and point ⁄⁄

Barefoot in the Dark

Coming downstairs, barefoot, in the dark
I head for the fridge, a yoghourt maybe,
and tread in something squelchy on the floor
cold, wet, and semi-solid.
lights!
cat vomit!

I add it to my list of
"Things The Cats Have Brought Us":
a slit frog, hundreds of feathers,
most with blood on them,
a whole wing, the body never found,
a dead vole tucked lovingly between the sheets
we discovered in the morning,
and several half dead birds it was the devil to catch
once they'd been pried from proud and puzzled jaws
and panicked round the room;
and fleas, and worms, and mice,
a rat behind the arras
and random, unidentified remains.

There are things you bargain for
and things you don't.
Considered coldly, these cats
tread as we do, tiptoeing in the dark,
hiding a precarious balance
between nine lives and nine deaths,
the expected carpet and the unexpected slime. //

On Being Led Back to the Youth Hostel, Blindfold, from the Pub

Warm evening air, the sound of occasional traffic, sheep,
and under my feet, grass, and stones, and mud,
grass again, marsh, until I wonder what route
I am taking, what precipice or soaking threatens
beyond my blindfold; I grip my daughter's hand,
learning to let go.

She, leading her father back from the pub,
near helpless with laughter, yet solid as blood,
guides me steady through the twilight,
across streams, through bracken, avoiding roads,
walls, low branches,
arriving triumphant, untying the scarf
"Daddy, we're here!".

Much trusted daughter, though you led me
through a marsh to tease me,
teetering from tussock to tussock
absurd, blind and fretful,
know, it is an unfeigned expression of love
to trust unseeing, and to accept that trust. ⌀

Standing Further Back

A child's death cankers our dreams
imaging the shape of our fears
for we know, but cannot know,
how, sudden as an earthquake

we are thrown into the pit of loss
never to escape, never again to see light
but from a deep shadow,
the world, but from another place.

And yet, as she works the lock gates
walks close to the seething edge,
what can I do but smile and watch -
she drowns imagination's hopes, with more imagining.

Prey to whatever preys on children
she sings and dances in the sun
her trust and beauty, that offend evil
subject to darkness.

She will, I know, grow up, she will survive -
harder for me to put my fear aside
and stand further back from the edge than
I could reach in the time it takes to drown. ⁄⁄

School Trip - The Essay

Bored, we stumbled over tree roots,
climbed beside waterfalls, and then
ate crisps and choccy bars high on the tops,
backs to the view.

Walking in the woods was boring,
even the sun, diamonding through leaves,
even the bright, poisonous mushrooms
even the mist hanging in the trees.

And how dull was that valley, with its patterned walls,
its sheep like toys from the high moor,
the drab play of light and water, the intricacy of insects,
the stultifying acres of the sky.

We battered on along a high cliff
and gulls, with wings outspread above us,
rode the cold wind.
And there was a sunset, later,
with all the lines of waves flecked gold across the bay
and Midas' golden dog, snapping at the foam.

Some say our souls are richer -
that however wet and bored and cold we seem to be,
inside, the rainbow and the rose will be remembered -
this essay bores me, my mind's a blank, the trip was shit,
 - though maybe the golden dog was fun,
the deadly, beautiful, toadstools
                              intriguing. ✍

Rights of Way

The map says there is a path here:
a dashed green line links this road with another,
evidence of old desires now cooled,
but nonetheless this signpost marks the start;
only, someone has ploughed where we need to walk.
A gate is locked, no stile,
and the next field impassable with rape,
tough stalks preventing;
our clothes roughly stained with pollen.
Are we right – and in the right ?

For England is not a wilderness: this is a patchwork
where every stitch has some intent:
footpaths, bridleways, boundaries, quilt the map;
the past is not easily ploughed out or planted over
the record stays.

We persevere, the path resumes,
our navigation vindicated by a fingerpost
just where we need it.
And now we join the story of these fields,
now the clods bear our mark, the bent stalks'
violation a droit de seigneur. ⁄⁄

Hurtling South

Hurtling South across the wide lands of Eastern England,
there's Spring in the air. Slews of sun glint
on wet fields, the afternoon brightens from grey and rain -
and we surprise a flock of rainbows.

Out to the East they glimmer, they shimmer, they leap,
one after another, mile after mile, span
from crock to crock. Who knew
how much treasure lay beneath these fields,
these tump-set farms, these brief-glimpsed villages,

or what benison a sky splattered with showers and sun
confers upon us travellers, trapped by the shining rails,
but carrying this beauty into the dark, forgetful city
beyond the end of the light. ⌇

Paradise

We all have our Paradise - or I hope we do.
There's a high road above Dentdale
where curlews fly winter and summer
and spread below the small fields enclose the light,
sheep pattern the varying green
and roads and streams lead their winding, rock-determined way
towards quiet places.

Peace; though here too
I have shouted with exhilaration when a blizzard's
whipped down the the valley from the east
feathering visibility to a few yards
for a few five-minutes; and then sunshine,
and the Howgills, ten miles away,
clear as a summer dawn.

Memory encompasses
dry seasons, when we walk and jump
the plates of rock in the river bed
and harebells line the way to Blea Moor;
there are orchids, and dippers,
and the rustling of small birds.

Autumn comes, overwhelming with brilliance;
and then Christmas, when the thin ice splinters
on the tractor ruts, and I strap holly to my pack
to walk home in the sun's last horizontal rays.

Gather ye holly while ye may;
the dale goes on, and these paths,
made by generations of farmers, shepherds and churchgoers
will endure beyond my feet.

Paradise endures,
and what healing lies in these few miles:
the resilience of landscape,
the diagnosis of light,
the cut of wind and sun
and the homeopathic glimpse of wrens.

That little bit of God in me;
that little bit of God in them. //

Farmer

We climb through his fields,
through lush grass from a wet summer;
through thistle, clover, dock, sheep droppings.
And here a ring that will grow fairies later;
and there a dip, nettled, its stone quarried.
The hedges are no longer laid, yet tidy,
and the walls rebuilt, made strong –
his sons did that.

But the soil is what matters:
clover, dung, grass, ploughed in
for wheat in another year.

And if he notices the two hares that start
under our feet and run, gracefully
ignored by the dogs, he does not say so.
Nor, as we reach the top, does he comment
on the half of Yorkshire spread out
beneath the roiling clouds, stabbed with sun spears,
and on the purple moor, the tidy villages,
the myriad fields, each with its own warden
resolutely keeping his eyes on the earth,
though his head be next to heaven. ✍

Bicycling on the Moors

Slowly, pedalling mostly, but pushing
on the steep bits, I climb onto the moor.
Sentinels, rooks stand by their nests,
shiny in bare watchtowers; a hare
sits in a field, and higher, larks rise
from the heather and tufted grass,
choralling madly in the eye of the sun.

Along the ridge, wind ruffles tormentil,
and marked stones and unmarked tumuli
stud the moor with lost importance. Below, farms,
knots at the junctions of hedge and wall
stitch the fields together, and the crazy clack
of tractors warps and woofs the land.

This is not Paradise – a barn sags ruined;
a kestrel darts low, and fatal; the windows
of village shop, school and pub are blind;
a crow picks eyes from a dying rabbit.

This is the country. How it became so
is a story we could discover – glaciers and wind and water,
man's digging and chopping, ploughing and shaping,
his need for constant movement, for shelter, food,
and quietly, unbeknown to the makers, to manufacture beauty.

It is what we have made it:
the cities, fields, and forests bear our mark.
We have worked with the Earth;
beauty and utility are in the blood,
and we have sometimes shown respect, and love
for what surrounds us – traits that may save us yet.
This is the practice to follow, the promise to keep. ⁄⁄

The Boundary

And was this the border of Elmet,
a ridge, defensible, stretching up
from the washlands
with their stocks of winter geese,
of ducks, a hunter's harvest;
and did it protect too, the ford
where the Romans later set their stamp
and left their name?

I walk this path and with one step
straddle two counties, can follow by eye
the line that links the highest points,
that picks up features
no-one would know (or care) how old they are,
indifferent as the kestrel that glides
from the field into the wood, targetting
some small rustling in the next kingdom.

Our world, ordered from remote offices
was carved by men with ploughs and axes,
smoothed by women planting, harvesting,
teased from one where kestrel, goose and duck,
took their territories from distant gods
who also made the hills, the rivers, and the ice. ⁄⁄

Hardy Revisited

Only a man harrowing clods
  In a slow silent walk
With an old horse that stumbles and nods
  Half asleep as they stalk.

Only thin smoke without flame
  From the heaps of couch grass:
Yet this will go onward the same
  Though Dynasties pass...

  From: In Time of 'The Breaking of Nations' by
Thomas Hardy. 1915.

I wonder. The vines creep northward,
the fields, once defined by hawthorn, oak and elm,
grow larger, and relict trees throw bare branches
against a sky where no larks sing or raptors fly.

Not dynasties pass, but decades only;
and while salmon return, so come the alien wasps,
the fungus that eats the bees,
the long slow perishing of marsh and moss.

Seen from the train, there still exists a countryside
Hardy would have loved. No working horses, true,
but on the hill, a church, a rookery, an ancient mound,
allowing the pretence that all is well. ⁄⁄

Love Poem

They came to the stepping stones, and crossed over.
They clasped hands, they planned each step,
they paused. It took an age;
but they had come to see the stream renewed
and diamonds flashing as they always had
on the dragonfly-kissed water.

They looked again at Paradise, and knew.

"We had a little walk," they said. But in that long slow morning
had seen death in Eden, had crossed the river for the last time. ⁄⁄

49

Easter Frost

Next door, children rush shrieking to find the eggs
and in our tree squirrels chase and blue-tits perch
while sun and wind contend the season.

We lie entwined. We know what lies behind the sky
for, wrapped in a duvet, long before dawn
we watched the comet hang above the trees,
plummeting around the sun.

And then, aroused by mystery and chill
we made love, and slept, and now warm and waking
I kiss your forehead, and stroke your hair
while fate burns in your eyes.

Gravity, attraction, light, combine here.
Our search is done, our Spring unfurled,
defying frost. ⁄⁄

The City

So it's a city you want -
I'll make a city for you.

To start, here are a million people
offered you like an unexplored galaxy;
new worlds of beauty and danger
begging acquaintance - in my city for you.

Adrenalin hustles,
dancers jostle in a thousand nightclubs,
concertos are played, buskers sing and juggle
and Dylan croaks from an open skylight
(don't think twice it's alright).
Every day is a symphony -
and the lost saxophone finds a home
in my city for you.

There are railings and fanlights, a policeman singing,
flowers outside a pub, and cats asleep.
Strippers, with their neat cases,
a white bicycle by a canal,
a concierge sweeps carefully,
and almshouses sleep in a flowery court.

There are ancient churches, modern theatres,
clothes drying up a close,
a river, corner shops, pavement cafés,
sculptures at bus stops and poems in stations,
and for me, trams,
and jazz in the park.

In summer it's hot, in my city for you:
there's dust in your face, lovers kiss and embrace
on every greenspace
while in the taxi-snarling streets
the tar melts and people turn ugly with the heat.
Rubbish stinks through into Autumn
when leaves stick to your shoes,
starlings swirl in orange evenings
and fog brings mystery to squares and crescents -
arachnid beauty in a silver sphere.

Your city will freeze you in winter;
it will lash you with rain and hail;
its skyscrapers will funnel weather at you.
It will sparkle with lights and Christmas windows,
with tinsel and trash,
and then surprise you, one morning, with quiet and snow.

Later, I offer crocuses, forsythia,
a thrush, daffodils in tiny gardens,
and high from a mansard room
(a chair, a table, and a single vase)
a haze of rooftops in the morning sun.

If it's a city you want
I'll make a city for you.

Your city will have players and orchestras,
folk clubs and rock clubs, rooms above pubs,
an art collection, and tiny galleries
where delicate objects wait for people to love them.
It will have broad avenues for vast crowds,
parades and celebrations, national mourning -
and quiet corners
where some live out their lives slumped and lost,
lovers tryst, and people who are not lonely but alone
take meaning for their quiet lives.

All this, and your dreams - in my city for you

and, of course, friends,
for sorrow, and increasing joy,
and to offer love. ⁄⁄

Grandad and the Winter Horses

Slowly along the house-lined street
and past the pub. The track gets rougher.
Walking's a new skill; she stops,
she examines a stone, considers a puddle.

On the town's edge is where the horses are,
the racks of hay, the scattered jumps,
a frozen cistern, horses begging in ragged coats.
They amble over.

We have no food, but I lift her towards the long face,
the large eyes, the tangled mane, the opposable ears.
It snuffles, whickers - long, shuddering, head-tossing
nose-curling, throat-clearing loud horse-talk.

She startles, eyes wide for re-assurance, grabs tight.
I laugh, hug; I'm not frightened.
But that's enough, she's trotting down the path
to another gate, another horse.

She stops, she looks, she bends her knees,
then, lip-flabbery, head-waggingly, tongue-spluttery, she snickers,
she snorts, she sways, she invites conversation.
The horse eyes her, says nothing. Its ears swivel.

She tries again. I choke on a laugh. Suspicious,
she glares, she stomps back on the path and heads home.
It's not amusing. You have to communicate.
Language is just around the corner.

At tea, I nicker, whinny, flabber my lips, slobber,
telling her parents. She looks on astonished.
I tell her: Grandad knows
there are some stories
you just can't tell with words. ✍

The Stepping Stones

One by one they cross the stepping stones,
with increasing confidence.
This year, the oldest helps the middlest,
next, the youngest needs help –
soon, they will be falling in,
relishing the familiar surprise.

Dams can be built, siblings splashed,
sticks floated down to be caught
as they hurtle through the gaps,
hand and eye together, like a heron fishing.

Now they come back, with their lovers, children;
soon they will be bringing us, helping us,
smiling to remember their own hesitant beginnings,
patient as we were.

I hope they will one day scatter
our ashes in the pool; watch
as they quicken between the stones,
grant us our little part in Paradise. ⁄⁄

Travelling On

No news forthcoming
I travelled on. Past the wintry fields
not yet snow-covered, but dun, wet,
past a pheasant at the edge of a wood,
red berries, a horse in a blanket;
the tower of Sherburn lost in mist,
headlights on the A1,
my mind there, and not there,
aware, yet unaware.

And at some moment that afternoon,
as the train took the bank
between Fenton and Garforth,
my grandson Arthur was born;
perhaps as we crossed the border of Elmet,
climbing out of Deira in the near dark.

Before I got the text, I was in Leeds.
Joy confined in an office, in a meeting,
the little screen my only link,
until on the way home,
hurtling back across the old kingdoms,
I could contemplate a new ruler
of my heart. ◢

A Window on the World

It's dusk, when orange, red, and purple
pulse in the west, the sky pitted by sodium,
and headlights, tail-lights stack at junctions;
when the lights come on in houses
in back rooms seen from the train:
kitchens, televisions, an unmade bed,
already some Christmas trees.
Here a woman lays a table,
children do homework,
and there, a man in a vest, a cat sleeping.

We pass in the night like Bede's sparrow,
granted a glimpse of warmth and feasting,
though whether to celebrate a birth,
or mark a death, is not revealed.

And what do they make of us,
staring into darkness like astronomers,
seeking the meaning of life
from the fleeing galaxies, a purpose,
a pattern, a reason for it all.

Faster, we enter a dark country.
By the time we look again,
those other worlds are gone,
the next town shut off by nets and drapes
from the prying eyes of aliens.
Just as well; too long a clip of other people's lives
encourages despair – the lights grown dim,
benighted, lost. We rocket on, our own reflection
all there is to contemplate. ⁄⁄

More Than We Thought

Back in the day, at the Renaissance,
Jupiter had four moons. That old heretic,
shaker up of cosmic theories, of God,
of hierarchy, of man the pinnacle of creation,
Galileo, spied them with his glass.

And I've seen them, through a small reflector,
watching them dance from one night to the next,
changing places, strung in a line,
as the great gas planet crept bright across the sky.

Now, it seems, those four are just the tip
of an iceberg of frozen worlds, more every year,
till we're counting sixty-five, sixty-six,
more than there are names for.
Callisto, Io, Ganymede, Europa, lost in the crowd.

The Earth has one. What a different
store of verse we'd have if four or 10
or 66 moons sailed through our night.
How must we think of ourselves, third planet out
from a single star, with a single moon,
now that we know every time we look,
there'll be another moon of Jupiter and,
out in the galaxy, another water-bearing planet
shines in the spectroscope, adding to
our wild surmise, our search for things like us. ⁄⁄

Progress

cutting down the conifers in our garden
revealed dancing boughs, squirrels, magpies,
an explosion of leaves, a world of light
wind-ruffled

like stumbling out of our Northern forests
into the Renaissance ⁄⁄

Cycle Racing – Minor and Major Themes

I

Thunder over Wales –
the sky dark as a volcanic cloud
shot through with lightning.

I fled, outpacing from Bridgnorth
the first heavy drops, head down, pumping the pedals,
winged by the roiling wind, racing to Wolverhampton.

And at last, as I bought my ticket, rods of rain hit the station
and all through the flayed landscape towards Birmingham
the lightning flashed on strange-hued ponds, cobalt, green,
    and crumbling walls.

II

On the film clip, a lone cyclist races the tsunami,
the 'copter shot shows tumbling ships, cars,
and buildings on fire, pursuing.

Churning in the wave
there will be the invisible, dislocated, flailing
bodies of the lost.

Legs failing, heart bursting,
the land flat, the overwhelming sea
unbounded. ⌐

Inside the Beltway

Saturday morning, Washington suburb;
the Beltway grinds behind the trees,
eight lanes, ten ? I don't count,
it's too much, too different.

But at the neighbourhood pool
it feels normal – Moms, Dads, on kid-duty,
watching, shouting, helping at the gala.

Kids eager to compete,
begging results from the judges,
burgers and coke from the café, sunshine.

Yet this is the country of Newtown, of Columbine,
where every school has lock-down practice,
where teachers cram kids into cupboards
and practice not breathing.

I'm amazed.
I could walk in here with a gun,
spray bullets round till the pool turns red,
till the grass would be slippery with blood.

How many parents have guns beneath their
t-shirts? Who could take me out ?
I don't see any.

I see a neighbourhood more trusting than
I had imagined, more determined
that violence will not rule their lives:
not quite the America we Europeans imagine,
not quite the America we Europeans fear. //

Pruning Roses

There's a knack, a skill,
and it's not hard –
though after, magical.

You cancel the future, it seems,
casting aside all signs of growth,
beheading low down so there's nothing left
except sticks, stuck in the earth like a hand of bones.

Give it a month
and a pink bulb appears below the scar,
greens at the base and feathers
into red-brown leaves.
The lopped rose grows again.

Is this how it works ?
The French Revolution cutting off the crown
so the citizens can flourish,
the Czar sacrificed for the proletariat,
Saddam dragged from his cellar,
Gaddafi from his drain,
and King Charles' life blood given to the Commons ?
Is this how it works ?

Some days, I'd like to think so,
but we don't any more massacre our rulers
once elected by the people,
however unjust, selfish, greedy and corrupt,
pursuing their war on the poor and needy.

We know how to prune roses and dictatorships,
We need to learn how to prune democracy;
have it grow again from its roots. ⁄⁄

Biking through Michigan

Today we biked through Michigan again,
wheeling again the long straight roads,
and racing the farm dogs, that curse and snarl,
stopping to photograph strange flowers,
corn-stubble rows, the cider mill,
its product translucent, amber, still.

Thirty-five years ,thirty-five years in which
our children have been born and grown;
your father's farming cousin, stooped and old,
alone with pigs and chickens then,
has died; your father too, who loved
the small towns, the silos, the red barn farms,
the wood-framed house his father built.

We have come back. These roads
lead back to our youth, your heritage;
these country graveyards hold your ancestors;
these scattered farms that once were theirs
after they, like you, had crossed the seas,
determined to start over.

Today we revisited foundations.
Today we biked through Michigan again. //

Country Roads, Michigan, USA

The dirt roads are still roads, but not dirt;
the family farm's still a farm, but not family;
and off this once dirt road the white-sided church
doesn't any more christen, confirm, marry us
though, round the back, they still bury us,
our name among others: Schairer, Schaibele, Jedele, Frey,
lined up against the fields and rows of corn we farmed,
the long stripes of the plough, the pockets of scrub we never cleared.

We are still here, but not farmers;
we sit behind a screen in Jackson, or Toledo,
weld the cars in Flint, in Dearborn,
drive the Interstate from client to prospect
chasing the sale - we the invisible.

But take your lunch at Metzger's, Hoffman's, Dieterle's – you'll
        find us,
our German faces, our German stockiness,
our not quite lost German accents,
 – retired farmers and farmer's sons,
shooting the breeze, touching hands;
and we are the harvest of all those generations,
watching Fox News in the subdivisions our farms have, or will,
        become. ⁄⁄

Learning to Breathe – a bicycle ride in May

At first it's terraces, then semis, shops,
the barracks, the college, the village on the edge
and then, passing the last house, the wet lane,
puddles at the side, hedges a-sparkle.

Now I'm no longer hobbled, hooded, kennelled, chained;
fields and sky widen with every turn of the wheel;
I am the lark ascending;
I sing !

This is how freedom feels;
this is when nine to five falls away
the suit, the tie, the brief-case for the brain
grow dusty in the wardrobe.

Nothing now between me and wild
possibilities unrolling along sunlit byways;
the track through the woods, the lane to the sea;

time to explore, time to stop, to wonder ...

People who are oppressed
call it Spring when they learn to breathe. ⁄⁄

Happiness

When it came, it flowered.
It stole up, like the wren in the bushes,
swung joyfully, like the finch on the niger seeds,
burst forth new leaves, like my daughter pregnant.

It felt crisp, like the cool edge of a sunny day;
but close as shared experience.
Happiness blossomed as I sat
in the summerhouse, one afternoon.

So this is it, I thought, not pursued, but a gift,
not a right, but a privilege,
and to be treasured as such.
Someday, it may come again. ⁄⁄

Operations, Procedures

Suddenly we are living with new vocabulary:
operations, procedures,emergencies,
superbugs, stomas, stents,
drains, scans, and septicemia,
scars, x-rays, anxieties, words:
malignant, insomnia, incurable,
cardiac, consultants, diagnosis,
nurses, rehab, going home,
palliative care, living
with death.

Eternity, afterlife, peace,
remembrance.

Is this how it's going to be
getting old ?
Will friends, colleagues, lovers, me,
one by one be caught
in this new web of words:
the scalpel and the infinite,
the intervention and the end of flesh. //

The Underground

There are tunnels beneath the hospital
where above, each building appears separate;
really, they are just the surface flowering of
routes for orderlies, the ways doctors use
to escape the needy, the place nurses go
to weep; the last journey of the dead
echoes through here among the whoops and skirls
of dinner ladies, pharmacists, anaesthetists,
racing their trolleys; releasing the world
from its burden of sick humanity
in sunlit wards above – all we visitors see. ▨

Bridget

We're making progress, Bridget and I.
We're passing milestones, getting there,
or, in my case, getting back.

Her first yawn, her first smile,
her sleeping through the night,
her rolling over. Accomplishments!

My milestones come closer.
I walk to the bathroom unaided,
I wear real clothes to sit in bed.

And while Bridget learns to hold up her head
Her Grandad sheds his monitor, takes fewer painkillers,
enjoys the taste of food again.

Sure, I sit up before she does,
but she's out in the sunshine first, in Spring.
I walk the length of the ward, climb some stairs,

and then I can go.

Now I'm outstripping Bridget - it's easy for me –
I've learnt it all before, I'm just re-activating
old patterns. For her, life is new.

I imagine her triumph at her
first steps; I'll be proud with her
at her first word, at her first stairs.

I walk to the coffee shop, next day to the pub,
I'm washing up, I'm making tea, ironing.
I'm back on my bike. It's all

a small miracle. For without the ambulance,
the careful butchery, the stitching up,
Bridget's ninth day might have been
the last milestone I ever saw her pass. ⁄⁄

Going Through

after all, it wasn't terminal:
on the other side there was another city
mirroring mine.
already I am in its suburbs,
abandoning the last stirrings of regret,
heading with what exhilaration, what fear,
what gathering speed,
into the unknown country
along remembered tracks. //

Other anthologies and collections available from Stairwell Books

First Tuesday in Wilton	Ed. Rose Drew and Alan Gillott
The Exhibitionists	Ed. Rose Drew and Alan Gillott
The Green Man Awakes	Ed. Rose Drew
Fosdyke and Me and Other Poems	John Gilham
frisson	Ed. Alan Gillott
Gringo on the Chickenbus	Tim Ellis
Running With Butterflies	John Walford
Late Flowering	Michael Hildred
Scenes from the Seedy Underbelly of Suburbia	Jackie Simmons
Pressed by Unseen Feet	Ed. Rose Drew and Alan Gillott
York in Poetry Artwork and Photographs	Ed. John Coopey and Sally Guthrie
Taking the Long Way Home	Steve Nash
Chocolate Factory	Ed. Juliana Mensah and Rose Drew
Skydive	Andrew Brown
Still Life With Wine and Cheese	Ed. Rose Drew and Alan Gillott
Somewhere Else	Don Walls
Sometimes I Fly	Tim Goldthorpe
49	Paul Lingaard
Homeless	Ed. Ross Raisin
Satires	Andy Humphrey
The Ordinariness of Parrots	Amina Alyal
New Crops from Old Fields	Ed. Oz Hardwick
Throwing Mother in the Skip	William Thirsk-Gaskill
The Problem With Beauty	Tanya Nightingale

For further information please contact rose@stairwellbooks.com

www.stairwellbooks.co.uk
@stairwellbooks